SAVING OUR WORLD

GENETICALLY MODIFIED FOOD

Nigel Hawkes

Franklin Watts
London • Sydney

© Aladdin Books Ltd 2000
Designed and produced by
Aladdin Books Ltd
28 Percy Street
London W1P 0LD

ISBN 0–7496–3719–6

First published in Great Britain in 2000 by
Franklin Watts
96 Leonard Street
London EC2A 4XD

Printed in The U.A.E.

Editor: Kathy Gemmell
Designer: Flick Killerby
Picture Research: Brooks Krikler Research
Certain illustrations have appeared in earlier books created by Aladdin Books.
A CIP catalogue record for this book
is available from the British Library.

Author Nigel Hawkes is science editor for *The Times* newspaper in London. He has
written a number of science titles for children.

Consultant Dr Sue Mayer is director of GeneWatch UK, an independent group based
in Derbyshire, which monitors developments in the science, ethics and
regulation of genetic technologies.

ABOUT THIS BOOK

This book is divided into chapters that lead the reader logically through
this topic. First we discover what genes are and how genetic modification
began. We learn about where food comes from and about farming practices
past and present. We look at how genetically modified crops are produced
and at the different types grown. We examine the issues surrounding
genetic modification, its impact on wildlife and the safety procedures.
Finally we look at genetically modified food in the shops, and at how far
genetic modification technology goes.
Throughout the book are stimulating **Talking Points** that raise greater
awareness and provoke discussion about the important environmental
topics and issues covered in this book. These are further backed up
at the end of the book by a **Look Back and Find** section, where
questions test the reader's new-found knowledge of the subject and
encourage further thought and discussion.

CONTENTS

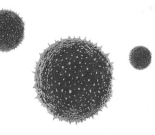

306644

Genetically Modified Food

New ways of making food

Scientists can now create plants that nature itself has never created – plants that are resistant to chemicals that kill weeds (herbicides), plants that produce chemicals to kill insects (pesticides) and plants that last longer after harvesting. The methods used to produce these new crops involve changing, or modifying, material within the crops, called genes. Genes are contained in the cells in all living things. They guide how living things are made and how they function.

Scientists analyse maize samples. By modifying the genetic material of maize or wheat, scientists can create new varieties.

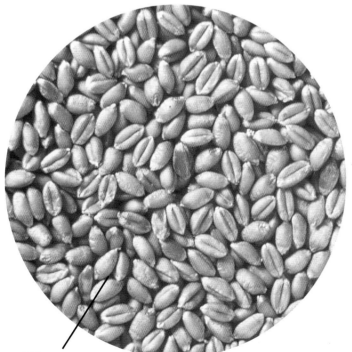

Wheat grains

A genetic engineer grafts a genetically modified sweet potato plant onto an indicator plant. The indicator plant will show if the modification has been successful.

GM food in the news

The production of genetically modified (GM) food is causing a huge row. Its creators believe that GM crops are the future of agriculture, and that they will be healthier and more productive than other crops. But many people believe the safety of these crops has never been properly tested, and that growing them may damage wildlife and the countryside. Health problems with other foods have left many people unwilling to accept what scientists claim. Some say that creating GM food is playing around with things we don't understand, and that the scientists have gone too far.

CHAPTER ONE

What are Genes?

The stuff of life

Genes are the recipe for all living things. They act as codes for different traits, such as the size or colour of fruit. These traits are passed from one generation to the next. Genes are carried in a chemical called DNA. Bacteria, which are tiny, one-celled organisms (living things), have their own supply of DNA. So does every cell that makes up every plant or animal.

Inside the cell, DNA curls up tightly.

DNA

DNA stands for deoxyribonucleic acid. Its secret lies in its structure – a long, ladder-like molecule that winds like a spiral staircase. The rungs of the ladder are made up of chemicals. The order of the chemicals along the DNA spiral forms a code that spells out the cell's job, just like the letters of the alphabet spell out the words in this book.

Each rung is made up of a pair of chemicals.

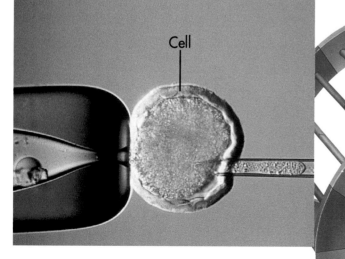

Cell

Scientists can inject DNA into cells using very precise microinjection instruments.

Chromosomes

In the nucleus (middle) of a cell (1) there are a certain number of chromosomes (2). Chromosomes are packages of tightly coiled DNA (3). In a human, the DNA in a single cell, stretched out, would be two metres long; in a whole body, this would make a hundred billion kilometres of DNA. All living things have chromosomes, though not all have the same number: humans have 46 per cell and tomatoes have 24. Half the chromosomes come from the father and half from the mother, so there are two copies of each chromosome, one from each parent.

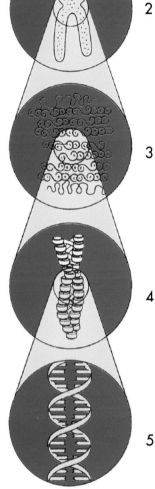

Genes are sections of DNA with special functions.

Genes

There are many, many genes (4) in a chromosome. Each gene is a section of the DNA spiral that is responsible for making a particular protein. It is the proteins that build the muscles and bones of all living things. Proteins determine what plants and animals look like and how they work. Seen close up (5), DNA looks like a double spiral.

TALKING POINT

There is an enormous number of genes in every single chromosome.

Q: What do genes do? Does each one have a special job?

A: Each gene is responsible for making a particular protein. Proteins make up the working parts of all plant and animal organisms.

How genetic modification started

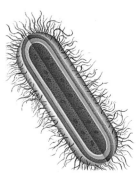

Escherichia coli

Scientists first learned how to alter the genes in an organism in 1973. The discovery was amazing and also alarming: for the first time, humans had new powers over nature. Before any experiments went ahead, safety precautions were put in place to try to stop people from using the new science in the wrong way.

▼ Swapping genes

The secret of swapping genes lies in rings of DNA called plasmids, which are found in bacteria. Plasmids seem to be nature's way of moving genes between different organisms. By cutting open the ring and putting in an extra piece of DNA – a gene – the plasmid's genetic message can be changed.

▲ Protein factories

The first experiments were done in bacteria called *Escherichia coli*. By modifying the plasmids in these *E. coli* cells and growing them in a special growth dish, they could be turned into bacterial factories able to make any protein. Different proteins are needed to build the different tissues of living things.

Plasmid

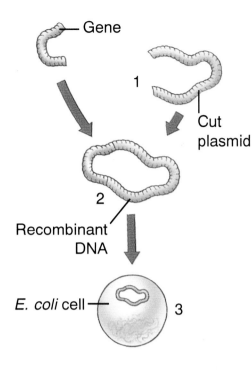

Gene

1

Cut plasmid

2

Recombinant DNA

E. coli cell

3

Growing bacteria

Bacteria modified using the recombinant DNA technique (above) can be grown in huge tanks full of nutrient broth in scientific laboratories. The added gene makes the bacteria produce a particular protein, such as insulin – a hormone – which can be taken out and used in human medicine.

◀ Cutting in genes

Plasmids can be cut open (1) using chemicals called enzymes. The cutting process leaves the plasmid with sticky ends. If another stretch of DNA – a gene – is added, it sticks and completes the ring (2). The result is called recombinant DNA. The new plasmid is then put back into the *E. coli* cell (3).

Scientists are trying to modify plants so that they produce proteins which can be used as medicines such as vaccines. The plants are grown in a nutrient broth, then put into containers in a growth room.

As well as making proteins, bacteria are also responsible for the germs and bugs that can make us ill. Recombinant DNA technology makes it possible, for the first time, to control bacteria.

Q: What if potentially dangerous modified bacteria escaped? Could they turn into superbugs and destroy life on Earth?

A: In 1975, at a conference in California, scientists laid down safety guidelines for modifying bacteria. No dangerous superbugs have so far been detected.

Farming Practices

Where does food come from?

Plants called cereal grasses – wheat, rice, barley, oats, maize and rye – provide about half of all the food energy we need. Animals also eat cereals, and we then eat the animals as meat. Together with fruit and vegetables, these make up our basic diet.

Cereal crops

How plants became crops

Ten thousand years ago, the first farmers began cultivating wheat because its seeds are good to eat when ground into flour and baked into bread. By finding the most productive plants and saving their seed to sow the next year, the farmers began to get bigger harvests. Over many years of selecting plants like this, crops began to differ from their wild ancestors.

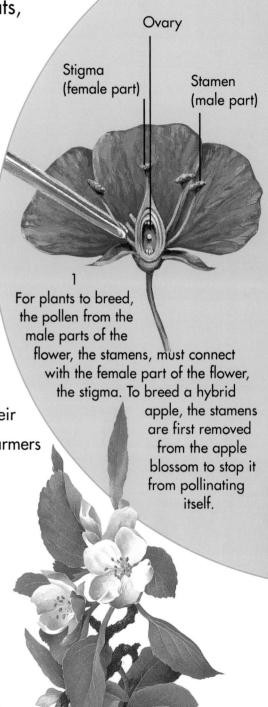

Ovary

Stigma
(female part)

Stamen
(male part)

1
For plants to breed, the pollen from the male parts of the flower, the stamens, must connect with the female part of the flower, the stigma. To breed a hybrid apple, the stamens are first removed from the apple blossom to stop it from pollinating itself.

Apple blossom can be cross-pollinated to produce hybrid apples.

Plant breeding

To further improve and vary food crops, farmers learned to cross one successful plant with another. This produced a hybrid plant that combined the best qualities of both plants. Hybrid crops are made by controlling the pollination of the plant's flowers (see the diagram above), but the plants must be closely related enough to allow cross-pollination to happen. High-yield (very productive) crops are grown in this way.

5 A hybrid apple is produced by cross-pollination.

Pollen tube

4 The pollen grains produce pollen tubes. One of these fertilises the ovary of the flower, which swells to become the new fruit.

3 The pollen is brushed onto the stigma of the first flower. The flower is then covered to stop other pollen from landing on it.

2 Pollen from the stamens of a flower on another plant is collected using a small brush.

Farming and society ▶

High-yield cereal crops and irrigation (large-scale watering of the land) have improved food production all over the world. But in some poor countries, farming methods and crop yields have changed little over the years.

TALKING POINT

About 300,000 years ago, humans lived by hunting and gathering. They killed animals when they could and collected nuts, roots and fruit to eat.

Q: Why did people start growing crops? Why have crop-breeding methods changed over the years?

A: People started growing crops so that they didn't always have to hunt or travel to find food. As populations grew, more people had to be fed, so farmers tried out new crop-breeding methods.

Q: Can you think of any foods that are still hunted today?

A: Fish and some wild animals. Some fish are grown in fish farms – large pens in the water – where they grow quickly because they are well-fed.

Modern farming

Today, huge amounts of food can be produced at low cost. This is made possible by farm machines, which can plough land and harvest crops far more quickly than traditional farming methods. The use of fertilisers to make crops grow faster and chemicals to kill weeds and insects has also increased the amount of crops grown. But modern farming has many critics, who say it can damage wildlife and the soil.

◀ Large-scale farming

Large-scale farming uses big fields, with chemicals to keep them clear of weeds and insects, fertilisers to feed the crops and machines to harvest them. Farmers on large-scale farms can grow up to twenty times as much food as their grandparents could on the same land. On intensive farms, animals such as chickens are kept indoors, warm and well-fed, so they grow faster.

Mountains of food

Intensive farming produces so much food that it cannot all be eaten. Some of this surplus food can be stored, but some has to be destroyed. Europe has regular surpluses of cereals, butter and meat. One reason for this is that farmers are paid a set price for what they produce, even if it is not needed.

◀ Subsistence farming

Many farmers in poor countries cannot afford chemicals or machines, and grow only enough to keep them and their families alive. They have only their muscles to work the land, or horses or oxen to pull the plough. This is called subsistence farming.

Organic farming ▶

Farmers who dislike large-scale or intensive methods may choose to farm organically. This means they still use tractors and high-yield crops, but avoid chemical sprays and fertilisers. They argue that the food is healthier and the soil is kept in better condition. Food that is organically grown is often more expensive because it is not produced in such large quantities as crops grown on large-scale farms.

TALKING POINT

While the developed world produces too much food, many poorer countries with subsistence farming produce barely enough to feed their people properly.

Q: Why aren't the food surpluses created in the rich countries given away to the poor countries as food aid?

A: They used to be, but it didn't work very well. Farmers in poor countries found they could not sell their own produce, so they stopped growing it. This made the poor countries rely even more on the rich countries for food.

CHAPTER THREE

GM Crops

How is genetic modification done?

Now scientists are going beyond using recombinant DNA in bacteria (see page 9). By adding new genes or stopping existing genes working, they can create crops that resist weedkillers, plants that produce their own insecticides, or tomatoes that go soft more slowly because the gene that makes them rot has been silenced.

1 The desired gene is chosen and isolated. This might be a gene that makes strawberries sweeter by producing more sugar.

2 The gene is cut into the plasmid of a bacterium called *Agrobacterium tumefaciens*.

6 The modified cells are encouraged to grow into plants, which are then planted in large nurseries to create more plants, or seed, for sale to farmers.

3 Cells are taken from strawberry plants.

5 The cells are tested to see which of them have been infected by the bacterium and have accepted the plasmid.

4 The bacterium containing the plasmid is mixed with the strawberry cells in a dish which contains a nutrient jelly to keep the cells alive.

◀ Microscience

Some plants, including cereals, cannot be modified by the *Agrobacterium* method. To modify these plants, genes are coated onto tiny gold pellets, which are then fired, like a shot from a gun, into plant cells. Some of the genes work inside the cells to produce a modified plant.

▼ The seedlings

Technicians working to produce new varieties of GM seeds must test the seedlings to see if the gene transfer has been successful. GM crops must also be tested in real farm conditions to make sure that they grow well.

With traditional plant breeding, scientists find plants with desirable traits, such as good growth genes, and cross them with crop plants. With GM crops, scientists cut or fire new genes into a plant's cells to produce a crop with the desired properties.

Q: How different are GM plants from plants produced by traditional methods?

A: Genetic modification is a more precise technique because it transfers just the desired gene rather than the many genes that get transferred in traditional cross-breeding processes. But even with GM crops, there is a risk of unexpected results. Scientists cannot be sure exactly where in the plant's chromosomes the transferred gene has gone. This may affect the way in which the plant grows and changes.

What is being grown?

The first GM crops to be sold were tomatoes, which were modified not to go soft so quickly. Then soya beans and oilseed rape – used to make oils (left) and margarines – were modified to survive certain herbicides (weedkillers). Maize and cotton were modified to carry a poison that kills pests and protects crops against damage.

Which crops?

GM crops have spread rapidly in the United States, but in some areas planting is being slowed due to public concern about the safety of GM food (see page 22). GM soya is the most widely planted, with GM maize also widely grown. GM oilseed rape and a few GM potatoes are also grown and so is GM cotton.

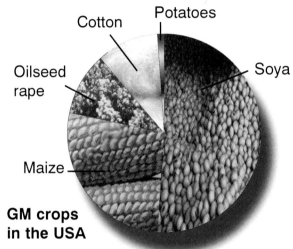

GM crops in the USA

Extended life

Tomatoes produce a chemical called an enzyme which makes them go soft after they have been picked. GM tomatoes are produced by turning off this enzyme, which means they stay firmer for longer. This gives them a longer shelf-life in the supermarket or at home.

Scientists adapt the ripening mechanism in a tomato.

Poison producers ▶

A bacterium called *Bacillus thuringiensis (Bt)*, which is found in the soil, produces a toxin (poison) that kills insects, but is harmless to people. Putting the *Bt* toxin gene into maize plants allows them to make their own poison, which kills a crop pest called the corn borer.

◀ Herbicide-resistant crops

Crops that can survive specially made weedkillers allow the farmer to spray the field without damaging the crop. All weeds and other plants die, but the crops do not. By decreasing the number of weeds, the farmer should increase the output of crops grown.

Type of modification ▶

By far the most common GM crops grown at the moment are those that resist herbicides (1). Second most common are the crops which can kill pests (2). Some crops have been given both these genes (3). Better quality crops and crops that have been modified to taste better (4) are not yet produced in large numbers.

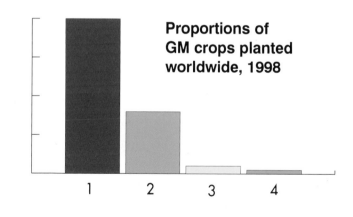

Proportions of GM crops planted worldwide, 1998

TALKING POINT

Fertilisers and pesticides are very widely used in modern farming.

Q: How does farming of GM crops affect the use of these chemicals?

A: By making crops resistant to pests, farmers should not need to spray fields so often. In future, some crops may make their own fertilisers to help them grow.

CHAPTER FOUR

The Issues

Why do we need GM crops?

Scientific farming has created the means to produce food to feed the world, so that nobody need starve. Supporters of GM crops believe that they are the next step, and say they will be able to grow in poor soil, with fewer chemicals, and will produce more nutritious food at lower cost.

◀ Drought-resistant crops

In future, GM crops that can grow in poor, dry or salty soils may be developed. This would make huge areas of worthless land productive, which would be a great boost to many poorer countries.

▼ End to starvation?

People starve because they are poor. Greater production of crops through genetic modification may allow more food to be grown in poor countries. GM rice containing vitamin A that can easily be absorbed by the body is being developed. Lack of vitamin A is a common problem in poor countries.

Aphids are common crop pests.

▲ Kind to nature?

Many crops depend on chemicals – pesticides and fertilisers – to make them grow. GM crops use gene biology to produce the same amount of crops using fewer chemicals. This may help nature by cutting down on the need to spray fields and use fertiliser.

◀ Healthy eating

Potatoes modified to contain less starch could make healthier chips because they do not absorb so much fat in the cooking. GM vegetables produced with added nutrients may help to fight off heart disease and cancer.

The companies ▶

A few big companies dominate the GM food production business. The companies that make the seeds also make the weedkillers that the plants need to be sprayed with. This means the companies benefit twice from GM crops: once from selling the seeds and once from selling the weedkillers. Critics say that the issue is too important to be left to the commercial motives of just a few big companies.

The weevil is a pest in potato fields. GM potatoes could be produced to kill the weevils that try to eat them.

TALKING POINT The GM food industry is big business. It employs many different people and involves many different organisations.

Q: Who is involved in the production of GM crops, and who does GM food affect?

A: Scientists, farmers, seed manufacturers, health experts, supermarkets, the public, environmental groups and even governments. They are all involved in either the production of the crops themselves, the buying of GM food or in the issues surrounding the GM food industry.

Effects on nature

GM plants could have unexpected effects on nature. The poisons intended to kill pests could damage other insects, while the genes put into the plants could escape in their pollen. Critics say that GM crops will encourage the creation of a sterile natural environment where no wild plants can flourish.

Huge fields of a single crop ruin natural habitats and squeeze wildlife into shrinking corners. GM crop fields may make this worse.

Dangerous toxins ▲

Laboratory experiments in the United States have shown that the *Bt* toxin intended to kill pests can also kill Monarch butterflies, which are harmless to crops. It is not yet known whether this would happen in the wild. Recent research has also shown that GM crops are leaking toxins from their roots into the soil. This may affect the goodness of the soil and may even produce new strains of pests.

▼ Cross-pollination

Pollen from GM crops may be carried a long distance by wind and cross-pollinate with wild plants or other crops. This may create odd breeds and upset organic crop farmers.

Pollen

Disappearing wildlife

To flourish, birds and the insects on which they feed need hedges, woods and areas of rough, weedy ground. Many songbirds are dying out in Britain because the habitat in which they live is being destroyed by modern crop farming. Otters are also endangered by lost habitat. Many people think that GM crops will make this worse. Others think GM crops won't make any difference to wildlife.

▼ Superweeds

Many people fear that if a gene that stops a plant being killed by a herbicide gets into a weed, it will create a superweed that will be difficult to destroy. Some scientists think that a superweed is likely to be rather feeble and will die anyway. But this needs to be proved before huge areas of herbicide-resistant crops are planted.

TALKING POINT

In crowded countries like Britain, wildlife habitats are being lost everywhere because of large-scale farming, drains, roads and houses.

Q: Does it matter if a few insects or birds disappear as a result of GM crops?

A: It may matter a great deal. Nature has a very delicate balance – different species rely on each other in ways that are hard to predict. Losing variety in nature is dangerous.

Safety procedures

People all over the world are thinking more about what they eat. Are GM foods safe? They might produce chemicals or trigger allergies in some people. But so might foods produced by conventional methods. Many people think that the only way to be sure that GM crops are safe is by careful testing and monitoring.

◀ Safety tests

Many people, including these scientists, believe that GM food is safe to eat. Others say existing tests don't prove anything – that too few plants have been tested over too short a time. Most tests have concentrated on the gene and what it does rather than on the whole food. Many GM crops are tested for safety on animals. Some early tests on experimental GM plants were worrying – they showed that lectin, which is a plant poison genetically engineered into potatoes, may have harmful effects on animals that eat them. More thorough testing is needed.

Learn by mistakes

Serious food mistakes can happen. In the 1980s, BSE (mad cow disease) spread through cattle in Britain, killing some people who ate the infected beef. The disease was caused by bad animal feed, but it took a long time to find this out. This experience has increased public worry about the possible long-term effects of GM food.

Allergic reactions ▶

In 1992, an American company put genes from Brazil nuts into soya beans to create a more nutritious bean. Some people are allergic to Brazil nuts. Tests showed they were also allergic to the GM soya. The project was dropped.

Health issues

GM crops may make food more nutritious by adding genes that produce more of the chemicals the human body needs for health and growth, such as vitamins. But there is a danger that the modification process might accidentally produce other chemicals which are damaging and whose effects may not be detected for a long time.

Protesters ▼

In some countries, trial fields of GM crops have been planted. Critics of GM crops say that these trials are dangerous and may harm the environment, and protesters have destroyed GM crops in the fields. Many scientists say that we need the trials to see how safe the crops actually are.

A protester paints a cross on his face to say no to GM crop trials.

TALKING POINT

In the United States, many GM crops have been planted with little opposition, until recently. But in Europe there has been a lot of protest.

Q: Why do Europeans seem to be more worried about GM food than Americans?

A: The United States is a large country with many wilderness areas where wildlife can survive. Europe is small and full of people, so wildlife and farming have to share the same space. Recent food scares in Europe have perhaps made people more aware about where the food they eat comes from. However, people in the United States are now becoming more and more concerned about the safety of GM crops.

CHAPTER FIVE

How Far does it Go?

GM food in the shops

By far the most widely used GM crop is soya, which is grown in the US, Canada and Argentina. Soya is used in many products, from soya oil to sauce thickeners. As a result of public worry about GM food, some producers and supermarkets do not use GM ingredients in their own brands, but GM ingredients are common in many foods.

Maize is used mostly as an animal feed. Soya beans are used as a source of oil, soya milk and lecithin, which is a thickener found in many foods, including chocolate. Many of the processed foods on supermarket shelves, including the ones below, contain soya which may be genetically modified.

Cereal

Sweets

Cake

Soya beans

Chocolate

Labelling

In Europe, all foods containing GM ingredients must be labelled so that shoppers know what they are buying. But labelling is very difficult – in some products, such as soya oil, no trace of the GM ingredient remains in the final food because it has been removed by processing. Many consumers are confused about what has GM ingredients in it and what hasn't.

GM ingredients

Although genetic modification technology still has far to go, it is possible to eat a lot of foods with GM ingredients in them. Pastries and sauces might be made with GM soya. In the United States, soups, pasta sauces and pizzas might contain GM tomatoes. One food ingredient that is commonly made from GM organisms is rennet, which is used in making cheese. Most cheese in Britain is made with GM rennet.

Tofu

Margarine

Pasta

Ice cream

Crisps

Bread

Baby food

Soup

Biscuits

Pizza

TALKING POINT

When GM tomatoes were sold in Britain, there were few protests because they were labelled so people had a choice.

Q: Why can't all GM products be labelled, so that people can choose non-GM food if they prefer?

A: Choosing non-GM food is hard because soya is such a widespread ingredient and most of the soya produced today is GM. Labelling is difficult because often there is no trace of the GM soya in the final food.

GM animals and beyond

Animals can be modified too, though none is yet used for food. Pigs and salmon have had genes added to make them grow more quickly. Sheep have been modified to produce drugs in their milk. Non-food plants such as cotton, tobacco and trees used for making paper have also been genetically modified.

Drugs in milk

Scientists in Edinburgh have added genes to sheep so that the sheep produce a particular protein that can be used in the treatment of some diseases. The protein is taken from the sheep's milk. This could be a cheap and easy way to make medicinal drugs.

◄ GM trees

GM trees that can be turned into paper easily have been created. But protesters believe that, like GM crops, GM trees threaten the habitat of tiny creatures in the bark, which may affect the way the forest's natural systems work.

GM fish

Salmon and trout with an extra growth hormone gene have been produced to grow four times faster than normal. Trials have proved that it works, but public opposition has so far stopped the fish from being produced on a large scale.

GM animals

Pigs have been modified so that, in the future, their organs might be able to be transplanted into human patients. But nobody plans to eat the GM pigs. So far, no GM animals of any sort are being used for food, although many animals are eating GM foods such as maize as part of their diet. Many people feel that humans do not have the right to interfere with the genes that make an animal an animal. Humans, after all, are also animals.

Animals can be genetically modified, but so far, no GM meat is being produced.

Most animals in intensive agriculture lead unnatural lives, far removed from their wild origins.

Q: Does genetic modification hurt animals?

A: It can do. Pigs that were given extra growth hormones suffered from arthritis in their joints, and the project was stopped. There are ethical limits on how we treat animals – what is acceptable for humans to do to animals, and what is going too far. These limits must not be ignored.

Look Back and Find

How much do you know about GM food? You can look back through the book to find answers to the questions on these pages. There are also some extra facts to increase your knowledge and make you think.

Genes

What are genes made of? What do they do? How do they store the information needed to build the proteins our bodies are made of?

A project called the Human Genome Project has worked out the sequence of every gene in the human body. This may help in making new drugs for treating disease.

Cereals

Which cereals do we live on? How might GM cereals be better?

Cereals are very productive crops, but they need a lot of food, in the form of fertiliser. One common fertiliser is nitrogen, which makes up 70 per cent of the air. But cereals cannot use nitrogen from the air, as some plants like beans can. A GM wheat that could do that would transform farming.

Farming

The world's farmers are not all the same. What is the main difference between farmers in rich countries and many of those in poor countries? What is the difference between organic farming and other kinds of farming?

In Europe, farmers produce so much food that it often has to be destroyed. To avoid this, sometimes farmers are paid not to produce food. This means they keep fields empty on purpose and still get paid as if they were growing crops there.

How genetic modification started

The first genetic modification carried out by scientists was on organisms called bacteria. How was it done? What kinds of product can GM bacteria create?

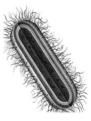

Genetic modification used for medicine has not caused the same problems or public outcry as GM crops. This may be because the technology is used to cure life-threatening diseases, and people can see the effects very clearly. However, some GM techniques – especially on animals – raise ethical questions on how far genetic modification should go.

GM foods

Which methods are used to genetically modify crops? Can you think of three GM crops on sale today? What do you think are the benefits of GM crops?

New methods are being used all the time. A new GM rice called golden rice is currently being developed. It contains beneficial vitamin A, which may help to improve diets in poor countries.

Large-scale farming

How do farmers in rich countries get the most from their land? What factors have made the most difference?

Modern farming has increased the amount of crops grown, but will it last? It takes ten calories of energy, mostly in the form of fuel, to produce each calorie of food. Farming using traditional methods needs only 0.1 calorie of energy per calorie of food, but it couldn't produce enough to feed everybody alive today.

Safety of GM food

How do we know if GM foods are safe to eat? How do we know if foods are GM or not? Are all non-GM foods safe?

In fact, many common foods are poisonous if eaten uncooked or in poor condition. Potatoes allowed to go green produce a toxin. Some nuts can kill people with a nut allergy. Do you think this means nuts should be banned?

The countryside

Some people are concerned that if anything goes wrong with GM crops it will be impossible to put things right. Others believe that GM crops will reduce the use of harmful chemicals.

Do you think that GM crops will make things better or worse for wildlife and the countryside? What risks should we be willing to take?

Genetic modification concerns

There are many concerns about GM foods. Can you make a list of them? How will people find out whether these concerns are important or not?

Knowing what problems may arise is one of the hardest things in science. Nobody expected that mad cow disease, BSE, would be spread by animal feed or that it would make beef unsafe to eat. The BSE crisis in Britain made a lot of people think more carefully about what they were eating.

Labelling

If people want to choose what they eat, why don't shops just label foods with GM ingredients and offer choices? What about foods that use GM ingredients in their production, but don't actually contain any because it has been removed in processing? Should these be labelled too?

In some countries, not labelling GM foods is against the law, but it can be hard to tell what has GM ingredients and what doesn't.

GM animals

Which animals have been genetically modified? And why? Are any of them available as food yet? Do you think that genetic modification of animals is right? If so, for what purposes?

Many people are worried that farm animals are already inhumanely treated and that their treatment is close to the limit of what is acceptable.

You Be Environmental!

Many environmentalists are against GM crops, seeing them as the latest stage in humans' abuse of nature. The effects of GM crops will depend upon how they are used. Some people think they will damage the environment, others think that if they need less weedkiller or insecticide, they might benefit wildlife. Future GM crops might help to feed growing populations, as past scientific developments in farming have done. But at what price? There are arguments for and against, and there may be good GM crops and bad ones. Look beyond the headlines and make up your own mind.

Useful Addresses

Friends of the Earth
26-28 Underwood Street
London N12 7JQ
website: http://www.foe.co.uk

Greenpeace
Canonbury Villas
London N1 2PN
website:
http://www.greenpeace.co.uk

Monsanto
(Life sciences and biotechnology company)
website:
http://www.monsanto.co.uk

Farmers find it hard to make a living and are often forced to farm every bit of their land, squeezing animals out. You can help by buying food at farmers' markets or in organic shops, rather than at supermarkets. Keep an eye on nature where you live, too. Are there fewer birds around your home than there used to be? Try to find out why. And try to leave some wild places in the garden for insects to thrive.

GLOSSARY

Agrobacterium tumefaciens
A bacterium used to infect plants and carry foreign genes into them.

Bacillus thuringiensis
A soil bacterium, called *Bt* for short, which produces a poison that kills insects.

Bacteria
Tiny living things, too small to see without a microscope and consisting of a single cell. Bacteria may cause diseases, but most are harmless. The singular of bacteria is bacterium.

Chromosomes
The packages in which genes are held inside a cell.

DNA
Deoxyribonucleic acid, the chemical which carries the information every cell needs in order to do its job.

Enzymes
Proteins in the body whose job it is to carry out chemical operations such as breaking up food in the stomach to digest it.

Fertilisers
Chemicals added to the soil to make it more productive. They can be inorganic – with chemicals in them – or organic, such as manure or compost.

Gene
A stretch of DNA containing the recipe for making a protein.

Habitat
The setting in which living things coexist, each playing its own part to maintain a balance. Examples of habitat are grassland and forest.

Hormones
Proteins which carry messages from one part of the body to another.

Nucleus
The heart of a cell, where DNA is concentrated.

Pesticides
Also called insecticides: sprays used to kill pests on crops.

Plasmids
Small rings of DNA that are found in bacteria. Plasmids are useful for ferrying foreign genes between organisms.

Pollination
The process by which pollen from one plant is carried to another, by insects, birds or wind, to produce seed with characteristics of both parent plants.

Proteins
The working chemicals of the body. Proteins consist of long chains of acids, curled up into complex shapes.

Recombinant DNA
The result of cutting and sticking a stretch of foreign DNA into a plasmid to make a new plasmid. Recombinant DNA technology is used to modify bacteria.

INDEX

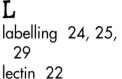

Picture Credits

Abbreviations: t-top, m-middle, b-bottom, r-right, l-left.

Cover & Pages 11, 12m & 24 - Eye Ubiquitous. 41 & 15b - Zeneca. 4r, 5, 16 & 27 - United States Department of Agriculture. 6, 12b, 18b, 19, 22, 23bm, 26b & 26-27 - Frank Spooner Pictures. 7, 17, 25 & 26t - Roger Vlitos. 8 both, 9, 13m, 15t, 23t & bl - Science Photo Library. 13t & 26m - Kathy Gemmell. 18t & 20 - Oxford Scientific Films.